Wheat Free Diet

Wheat Free Living with Delicious Wheat Free Recipes

Cristina Davis

Table of Contents

Introduction: What is a Wheat Free Diet

Basically, the wheat free diet means you no longer consume wheat products. Wheat, unfortunately, is in many foods on the shelves today in the grocery store. If you are truly going to go wheat free, you have to be diligent in reading labels. It helps to go homemade and that way you control exactly what goes into your meals.

A lot of talk goes on about being "gluten free" too. Gluten is a substance found in wheat, it is also found in other foods, though wheat is the largest gluten food. It helps to know exactly what wheat is and what gluten is. Gluten is a protein found in wheat, barley, and rye. Gluten is also found in alcohol and can contaminate foods like oats during the manufacturing process. Many processed (or convenient) foods contain gluten. Watch out for certain potato chips, soups, French fries (the frozen kind), cold cuts, and certain soups. Nowadays it is a big deal to label a product as "gluten free" so you may want to pay attention to this when grocery shopping.

If you go "gluten free," you are also going "wheat free."

Knowing this terminology will help while you are out and about in choosing foods at restaurants and at the grocery. This cookbook is "wheat free" meaning all the recipes within do not contain wheat ingredients.

Benefits of a Wheat Free Diet

A wheat free diet is very beneficial for people who suffer from wheat and gluten intolerances and allergies and celiac disease. It is also helpful for those with irritable bowel syndrome or other chronic intestinal issues. By going wheat free, you are helping to stop the allergies and intolerances caused by eating wheat.

By not eating wheat, you may help to improve your digestive function. For those with wheat intolerances, they have them because their body cannot properly digest the wheat. When they stop ingesting the wheat, the digestive system has a chance to heal and function improves. When wheat is present, it literally sticks to the walls of the digestive tract (in those who suffer with wheat intolerances). This slows down the digestive process, which can lead to bad bacteria growth and unhealthy digestive system. The results are unpleasant, bloating, flatulence, constipation, or diarrhea.

There are other benefits to going wheat free with your diet other than the obvious relief of digestive issues. Because wheat is found in so many processed and convenient foods (another way of saying 'junk' food) you will now have to avoid eating junk food. This means you are avoiding the preservatives, artificial colors and flavors (nice words for manmade chemicals). These foods are responsible for weight gain and a host of other health issues. So, you guessed it, a side benefit of going wheat free is weight loss. Also you lower your risk for cardiovascular disease and hypertension by not eating wheat laden junk foods.

Sometimes when people have wheat intolerances, they may not show digestive issues. It may show up in the form of arthritis, bone loss, joint pain, and autoimmune disease issues. This makes diseases like celiac disease hard to diagnose. But the good news here is that the benefits of a wheat free diet include more than just improved digestive function, it helps to alleviate the other issues associated with the condition such as those just listed. If you suffer from joint and bone issues, you may find a wheat free diet helps to improve your health.

Let us discuss one of the main reasons people go wheat free aside from helping against wheat intolerances, that of weight loss. Often, people who are diagnosed with wheat intolerances will find they lose weight when they adopt this diet plan. The diet has a lot to do with it because you have a healthy choice of vegetables, fruits, and lean meats instead of wheat products.

How to Eat a Wheat Free Diet

Going on the wheat free diet may seem frustrating at first, especially if you are accustomed to eating your fill of convenient and processed foods. Many carbohydrates are addictive foods, so going off them may cause a slight withdrawal. You may feel irritable and really want to reach for that packaged goodie. Resist the urge and instead fill your belly with healthy whole foods. If you are bad addicted to junk foods there are a few recipes within this book in the Appetizer, Dessert, and Snack Recipes section that has recipes that resemble the types of foods you may love, only these recipes are healthy made from nutritious whole foods.

You may mistakenly think you have to give up all breads and bread products. Not true, because, as you can tell from the Bread Recipes section in this book there are alternatives for creating delicious bread products. You may also find pre-packaged "gluten free" breads, baking mixes, cakes and cookies at your grocery store now, because it is becoming more readily available. However, because it is a specialty food it comes with a higher price tag. You may find that cooking your own food saves on your grocery bill in the long run.

Advice for Wheat Free Dieting Success

Watch all the foods you consume. Read the labels and be mindful of every bite you put in your mouth. The best bet is to go for foods that are whole foods, fresh foods, and you cannot fail.

Remember wheat products can sneak into foods, even if you think it is not. If you are out and about and sitting down at a restaurant, you may think ordering a salad will be safe. But be aware that even certain salad dressings contain wheat. The chunks of ham in the salad may contain wheat. The sauce on your spaghetti may contain wheat. That bowl of soup you get in a 4-course meal may contain wheat. All these foods seem innocent of having wheat, but in truth, if they are premade and processed, manufacturers like to include an abundance of cheap ingredients, wheat being one of them.

Find healthy alternatives to wheat products and make it from scratch. Wheat flours are an easy one to substitute. Look for rice flour, buckwheat (not a "wheat" product), rye, arrowroot, quinoa, amaranth, corn flour, oat flour. These are a lot healthier and though baking needs minor adjustments, it is done very successfully. The recipes within this book call for these ingredients; you can test these recipes to find out for yourself how good they really are.

Are There Risks To Eating Wheat Free?

The biggest risk is the nutrient deficiencies you may encounter if you are accustomed to eating "enriched" wheat products. Enriched means the wheat has added nutrients like iron, B vitamins, calcium, and such. If you stop eating this and you do not get it from another source, you run the risk of having a vitamin or mineral deficiency. The key to avoiding this is balance. Eat a healthy, albeit wheat free, diet. You should consume the foods that naturally have these nutrients. So keep a balanced diet, do not just stick with a couple of foods. Try to eat a wide range of vegetables, fruits, and lean meats and you will keep your body healthy.

Please note, the recipes within this book are recipes that have been around all over and are yet unique to this book but may be similar to others. Feel free to modify the recipes as you see fit. Who knows? You may create a masterpiece by doing so.

Sample 5 Day Menu

Feel free to add to the meal plan, adding eggs, and a meat with breakfast, and adding steamed vegetables and a salad with supper if desired. Beverages are your choice, though the best choices are fruit juice, tea, and water.

Day One

Breakfast - Blueberry Muffins
Snack - Nuts
Lunch - Buffalo Chicken Breasts Salad
Snack - Fruit
Supper - Grilled Shrimp, Brown Rice Apple Salad, White Bread
Dessert - Chocolate Cake

Day Two

Breakfast - Chocolate Peanut Granola, milk
Snack - Fruit
Lunch - Beef Stew, Cornbread
Snack - Nuts
Supper - Stuffed Peppers, Seasoned Green Beans, Cheese Bread

Dessert - Chocolate Pudding

Day Three

Breakfast - Fruit Salad with Yogurt Dressing
Snack - Spicy Nut Mix
Lunch - Chili, Cheese Bread
Snack - Fruit
Supper - Salmon Packets, Boston Baked Beans, Cornbread
Dessert - Five Layer Dessert Bar

Day Four

Breakfast - Strawberries and Cream
Snack - Fruit and Nut Cheese Ball with gluten free crackers
Lunch - Fruit and Brown Rice Dish
Snack - Spicy Nut Mix
Supper - Lemon Pepper Chicken, Oven Roasted Herbed Potatoes, Stuffing
Dessert - Orange Cream Sorbet

Day Five

Breakfast - Pumpkin Raisin Oatmeal
Snack - Peanut Butter Cookies

Lunch - Chicken Enchilada Casserole

Snack - Fruit

Supper - Mushroom Broccoli Quiche, Healthy Collard
Greens, Irish Soda Bread

Dessert - Cocoa Macaroons

2

Wheat Free Diet Recipes

Wheat Free Diet Breakfast Recipes

Blueberry Muffins

Here is a delicious wheat-free blueberry muffin, good hot or cold. Makes a dozen muffins.

What You'll Need:

2 eggs
1 egg yolk
1 1/2 cups of rice flour (white)
1 cup of rice flour (brown)
1 cup of blueberries
1 1/4 cups of milk
3/4 cup of sugar (granulated)
1/2 cup of butter
1 tablespoon of brown sugar
1 tablespoon of lemon zest (grated)
1 tablespoon of vinegar (white)
4 teaspoons of baking powder
1/2 teaspoon of salt

How to Make It:

Prep: Preheat the oven to 400 degrees Fahrenheit. Add cupcake liners to 12 muffin cups.

In a bowl, combine the 1 1/4 cups of milk with the tablespoon of white vinegar. Set aside. Meanwhile, in another bowl, using an electric beater beat the 2 eggs and egg yolk. Add the 3/4 cup of granulated sugar and beat for a minute. Add the vinegar milk and the tablespoon of lemon zest. Beat for another minute, scraping the sides. In a separate bowl, combine the 1 1/2 cups of rice flour (white), 1 cup of rice flour (brown), 4 teaspoons of baking powder, and 1/2 teaspoon of salt. Add to the batter slowly, stirring as you add. Fold in the cup of blueberries, carefully. Divide the batter into the 12 lined muffin cups. Add a pinch or two of the tablespoon of brown sugar on top. Bake for 20 minutes, until golden brown.

Chocolate Peanut Granola

This delicious granola is perfect with a tall glass of ice cold milk. Makes 8 servings.

What You'll Need:

2 1/2 cups of oats
1/2 cup of peanuts (raw, chopped)
1/2 cup of peanut butter chips
1/3 cup of cocoa powder
1/4 cup of chocolate chips (semisweet)
1/4 cup of chocolate chips (white)
1/4 cup of coconut oil
1/4 cup of honey
1/4 cup of sugar (granulated)
1/8 teaspoon of coconut extract
1/8 teaspoon of vanilla extract
Salt

How to Make It:

Prep: Preheat the oven to 275 degrees Fahrenheit.
Spray a small baking sheet with cooking spray.

Add the 1/4 cup of coconut oil to a saucepan and turn to medium heat. Add the 1/3 cup of cocoa powder, 1/4 cup of honey, 1/4 cup of sugar (granulated), and a couple dashes of salt and stir with a whisk. Stir in the 1/8 teaspoon of coconut extract and 1/8 teaspoon of vanilla extract. Turn the burner off but leave saucepan there. In a bowl, combine the 2 1/2 cups of oats, 1/2 cup of almonds (raw, chopped), and 1/2 cup of peanut butter chips. Stir in the warmed chocolate mixture, coating all pieces of chips and oats. Press into the small baking sheet. Bake for 50 minutes. Turn the oven off and leave pan in there for another half an hour. When cooled, bust the granola apart in a large bowl, toss in the 1/4 cup of chocolate chips (semisweet) and 1/4 cup of chocolate chips (white). Store in a tightly closed container at room temperature.

Fried Apples

This is a delicious breakfast food, eat as its own dish, or over toast or pancakes. Makes 8 servings.

What You'll Need:

4 apples (tart, cored, peeled, slices)
1/2 cup of brown sugar
1/2 cup of water (cold)
1/4 cup of butter
2 teaspoons of cornstarch
1/2 teaspoon of cinnamon (ground)
Raisins (optional)

How to Make It:

Add the 1/4 cup of butter to a large skillet and turn to medium heat. When the butter melts add the 4 sliced apples, fry for 7 minutes, stir continually. In a cup, combine the 1/2 cup of cold water with the 2 teaspoons of cornstarch with a whisk. Pour over the apples along with the 1/2 cup of brown sugar and 1/2 teaspoon of ground cinnamon. Turn to high and bring to a boil, stirring constantly, for a couple of minutes. Option, stir in a hand full of raisins. Serve immediately.

Fruit Salad with Yogurt Dressing

This is a refreshing breakfast made with fresh or frozen fruits and the wholesome goodness of yogurt. Makes 6 servings.

What You'll Need:

2 cups of yogurt (plain)
2 cups of strawberries (chopped)
2 cups of grapes (seedless, green, halved)
1 cup of blueberries
1 cup of raspberries
2/3 cup of bananas (peeled, sliced)
2 tablespoons of honey
1 tablespoon of orange juice
3/4 teaspoon of vanilla extract

How to Make It:

Add to a bowl, 2 cups of yogurt (plain), 2 tablespoons of honey, and the 3/4 teaspoon of vanilla extract and combine with a whisk. In a separate bowl combine the 2/3 cup of bananas (peeled, sliced) and the 1 tablespoon of orange juice. Stir in the 2 cups of strawberries (chopped), 2 cups of grapes (seedless, green, and halved), 1 cup of blueberries, and 1 cup of raspberries.

Drizzle the yogurt dressing over the top of the fruit and toss to combine. Serve immediately.

Healthy Ham Quiche

This is healthy because it is turkey ham, with less fat than regular ham, but just as delicious. Makes 1 large pie.

What You'll Need:

2 packages of frozen hash browns (12 oz each)
2 eggs
1 cup of Monterey Jack cheese (shredded)
1 cup of turkey ham (diced)
1/2 cup of heavy whipping cream
1/3 cup of butter (melted)
Salt and pepper

How to Make It:

Prep: Preheat the oven to 425 degrees Fahrenheit.

Remove the frozen hash browns from the bags and pat dry with a paper towel then mix them with the 1/3 cup of melted butter. Press the butter coated hash browns into a 10-inch pie pan. Bake for 25 minutes in the hot oven. Once the potatoes are out of the oven, add the cup of turkey ham on top of the potato crust, then sprinkle the cup of shredded Monterey Jack cheese over

the ham. Crack the 2 eggs and beat with a whisk.
Combine with the 1/2 cup of heavy whipping cream and
dashes of salt and pepper. Pour over the top of the
cheese do not stir. Bake for about a half an hour until
the eggs are set

Mushroom Quiche

The crust is made from quinoa so no worries of wheat in this delicious quiche. Makes a 9 inch pie.

What You'll Need:

7 eggs
2 scallions (chopped)
2 cups of mushrooms (chopped)
1 1/2 cups of broccoli florets (chopped)
1 1/4 cups of quinoa flour
2/3 cup of cheddar cheese (shredded)
1/2 cup of half-and-half
1/2 teaspoon of garlic (minced)
1/3 cup of butter (room temperature)
Salt and pepper
Water

How to Make It:

Prep: Preheat the oven to 350 degrees Fahrenheit. Spray a 9 inch pie pan with cooking spray.

Add the 2 cups of chopped mushrooms to a skillet and turn to medium, stirring for about 10 minutes. In a bowl, crack the 7 eggs and beat with a whisk. Stir in the

1/2 cup of half-and-half, then add the 1 1/2 cups of broccoli florets (chopped), 2 scallions (chopped), 2/3 cup of cheddar cheese (shredded), 1/2 teaspoon of garlic (minced), and dashes of salt and pepper. Last stir in the cooked mushrooms. Set aside. In another bowl, mix the 1 1/4 cups of quinoa with a little water, a teaspoon at a time, until it forms pie crust. Press into the prepared pie pan, and then pour the egg mixture into it. Carefully set it on a baking sheet and place in the hot oven and cook for a little over half an hour, until the eggs are good and set.

Pancakes

Add your favorite syrup or fruit topping to complete this breakfast favorite. Make 6 servings.

What You'll Need:

2 eggs
2 cups of water
1 cup of rice flour
1/3 cup of potato starch
4 tablespoons of dry buttermilk powder
3 tablespoons of canola oil
3 tablespoons of tapioca flour
1 tablespoon of honey
1 1/2 teaspoons of baking powder
1/2 teaspoon of arrowroot
1/2 teaspoon of baking soda
1/2 teaspoon of salt

How to Make It:

Combine the 1 cup of rice flour, 1/3 cup of potato starch, 4 tablespoons of dry buttermilk powder, 3 tablespoons of tapioca flour, 1 1/2 teaspoons of baking powder, 1/2 teaspoon of arrowroot, 1/2 teaspoon of baking soda, and 1/2 teaspoon of salt in a bowl. In a separate bowl beat the 2 eggs with a whisk then combine with 2 cups of water, 3 tablespoons of canola oil, and 1 tablespoon of honey. Mix the wet into the dry ingredients, batter will be slightly lumpy. Turn griddle or sprayed skillet to medium high heat. Drop a ladle full of batter onto the hot surface and flip with the edges start to bubble and the center is set. Cook on flip side until golden brown. Serve with your choice of toppings.

Pumpkin Raisin Oatmeal

This is delicious flavored oatmeal adds a little crunch to your morning. Makes 4 servings.

What You'll Need:

1 can of pumpkin puree (14 oz, natural)
2 cups of water
2 cups of milk
2 cups of oats (quick cooking)
1/4 cup of pumpkin seeds
2 tablespoons of raisins
3/4 teaspoon of pumpkin pie spice
1/4 teaspoon of salt
Honey
Butter

How to Make It:

Pour the 1 can of pumpkin puree (14 oz, natural) into a large saucepan and combine with the 2 cups of water, 2 cups of milk, 2 tablespoons of raisins, 3/4 teaspoon of pumpkin pie spice, and the 1/4 teaspoon of salt. Turn the heat to high and bring to a boil. Stir in the 2 cups of oats (quick cooking) and cook for the amount of time specified on the quick cooking oats container. Stir frequently. Add the 1/4 cup of pumpkin seeds to a skillet on medium heat, stir, and toast for 10 minutes. Serve the oatmeal by dividing into 4 bowls, add a pat of butter, stir, then divide the pumpkin seeds on top, and lastly add a drizzle of honey to each bowl.

Raspberry Peach Nut Yogurt

This is a delicious and nutritious way to start the day with fresh fruit, yogurt, and almonds. Makes 4 servings.

What You'll Need:

1 peach (peeled, diced)
4 cups of yogurt (plain Greek)
1 cup of raspberries
1/4 cup of almonds (toasted, sliced, + 1 tablespoon finely chopped)
1/4 cup of honey
1/4 cup of raisins
2 teaspoons of orange zest (grated)
1 1/2 teaspoons of vanilla extract
Peach nectar

How to Make It:

Combine the 4 cups of plain Greek yogurt with the 1/4 cup of honey, 2 teaspoons of orange zest (grated), and 1 1/2 teaspoons of vanilla extract. If too thick add some peach nectar until it reaches the desired consistency. Stir in the 1 peach (peeled, diced), 1 cup of raspberries, and 1/4 cup of raisins. Divide into 4 serving bowls. Garnish with the tablespoon of finely chopped almonds.

Strawberries and Cream

This is a slightly different twist on strawberries and cream, with a touch of balsamic vinegar gives a tiny bit of tangy, and the creamy smoothness of ricotta cheese, gives a flavorful cream. Makes 4 servings.

What You'll Need:

2 cups of strawberries (hulled, quartered)
1 cup ricotta cheese
4 tablespoons of honey (divided)
3 tablespoons of balsamic vinegar
2 tablespoons of basil leaves (chopped)
1/2 teaspoon of vanilla extract

How to Make It:

Add the cup of ricotta cheese, 2 tablespoons of honey, and the 1/2 teaspoon of vanilla extract into a blender or food processor and blend until smooth. Pour into a bowl, cover, and refrigerator for an hour. Pour the 3 tablespoons of balsamic vinegar and 2 tablespoons of honey into a small saucepan. Turn the heat to medium, and using a whisk, heat for a couple of minutes. Add the 2 cups of hulled and quartered strawberries to a bowl and toss in the 2 tablespoons of chopped basil leaves.

Pour the vinegar and honey over the strawberries. Spoon the ricotta cheese cream into 4 bowls and then top with equal divided amounts of the strawberries.

Wheat Free Diet Bread Recipes

Cheese Bread

This is a delicious bread, a perfect companion with a savory main dish. Makes 6 mini loaves.

What You'll Need:

2 eggs
2 cups of tapioca flour
2/3 cup of Parmesan cheese (grated)
1/2 cup of olive oil
1/3 cup of milk
1/3 cup of water
2 teaspoons of garlic (minced)
1 teaspoon of salt

How to Make It:

Prep: Preheat the oven to 375 degrees.

Place a saucepan on the stove and turn to high heat. Pour in the 1/2 cup of olive oil, 1/3 cup of milk, and 1/3 cup of water and bring to a boil. Remove from heat when boiling starts. Add the 2 cups of tapioca flour and the 2 teaspoons of minced garlic and stir. Set aside for 15 minutes to cool. Next, beat the 2 eggs then stir into the batter along with the 2/3 cup of grated Parmesan cheese. The batter will be slightly lumpy. Divide the dough and drop 6 equal sized "balls" onto a baking sheet. Bake for about 18 minutes, until the "bread" is golden brown and crusty.

Chocolate Cake

This is a delicious dessert for chocolate lovers. Makes one 9 inch cake.

What You'll Need:

4 eggs
1 1/2 cups of white rice flour
1 1/4 cups of sugar (granulated)
1 cup of milk
2/3 cup of sour cream
3/4 cup of millet flour
1/2 cup of cocoa powder
2 teaspoons of vanilla extract
1 teaspoon of arrowroot
1 teaspoon of baking powder
1 teaspoon of baking soda
1 teaspoon of salt

How to Make It:

Prep: Preheat the oven to 350 degrees Fahrenheit. Spray a 9 inch round pan with cooking spray.

Combine the 1 1/2 cups of white rice flour, 3/4 cup of millet flour, 1/2 cup of cocoa powder, 1 teaspoon of arrowroot, 1 teaspoon of baking powder, 1 teaspoon of baking soda, and 1 teaspoon of salt in a bowl. In a separate bowl combine the 4 eggs, 1 1/4 cups of sugar (granulated), 1 cup of milk, 2/3 cup of sour cream, and 2 teaspoons of vanilla extract. Gradually mix in the dry ingredients and stir until smooth. Pour into the prepared 9 inch round pan. Bake for about 23 minutes, until the top becomes springy. Cool on a wire rack. Remove from pan and top as desired.

Make a 2 layer cake by doubling the recipe.

Cornbread

Cornbread goes well with so many meals and is a staple with some dishes. Makes 1 9x9 inch pan.

What You'll Need:

2 eggs
1 1/2 cups of cornmeal (fine)
1 1/2 cups of water (warm)
1 cup of millet flour
1 cup of rice flour
1/4 cup of canola oil
1/4 cup of sugar (granulated)
1 tablespoon of baking powder
1 teaspoon of salt

How to Make It:

Prep: preheat the oven to 400 degrees Fahrenheit. Spray a 9x9 inch baking pan with cooking spray.

Beat the 2 eggs and mix with the 1/4 cup of canola oil, then stir in the 1 1/2 cups of water (warm). In a separate bowl, combine the 1 1/2 cups of cornmeal (fine), 1 cup of millet flour, 1 cup of rice flour, 1/4 cup of sugar (granulated), 1 tablespoon of baking powder, and the 1 teaspoon of salt. Gradually pour the wet ingredients into the dry ingredients and stir to moisten, do not over stir. Pour the cornbread batter into the prepared 9x9 inch baking pan and bake for 20 minutes or until the top turns a golden brown.

Irish Soda Bread

You will enjoy this bread with butter and your favorite toppings or alone. Makes 1 9-inch round pan.

What You'll Need:

1 egg
1 1/2 cups of rice flour (white)
1 cup of buttermilk
1/2 cup of sugar (granulated)
1/2 cup of tapioca flour
1 teaspoon of baking powder
1 teaspoon of baking soda
1 teaspoon of salt

How to Make It:

Prep: Preheat the oven to 350 degrees Fahrenheit. Spray a 9-inch round pan with cooking spray.

In a bowl, beat the egg, and then stir in the cup of buttermilk. In a separate bowl, mix the 1 1/2 cups of rice flour (white), 1/2 cup of sugar (granulated), 1/2 cup of tapioca flour, 1 teaspoon of baking powder, 1 teaspoon of baking soda, and 1 teaspoon of salt. Pour the liquid into the dry ingredients and combine well.

Pour the batter into the prepared 9-inch round pan. Bake until a toothpick inserted in the middle comes out clean, a little over an hour. Cool for 10 minutes on a wire rack. Store wrapped in foil or plastic wrap.

Pumpkin Muffins

Whether you eat these delicious muffins for breakfast or as a snack, it is entirely up to you because they are good no matter what time of day it is. Makes a dozen and a half of muffins.

What You'll Need:

1 can of pumpkin puree (15 oz)
3 eggs
1 1/2 cups of sugar (confectioners')
3/4 cup of white rice flour
1/2 cup of brown rice flour
1/2 cup of brown sugar
1/2 cup of tapioca flour
1/2 cup of butter (melted, divided)
1/4 cup of milk (plus more)
1/4 cup of sorghum flour
1 1/2 teaspoon of baking powder
1 teaspoon of cinnamon (ground)
1/2 teaspoon of baking soda
1/2 teaspoon of salt
1/4 teaspoon of cloves (ground)
1/4 teaspoon of ginger (ground)
1/4 teaspoon of nutmeg (ground)

How to Make It:

Prep: Preheat oven to 350 degrees Fahrenheit. Line 18 muffin cups with cupcake papers.

Combine the 3/4 cup of white rice flour, 1/2 cup of brown rice flour, 1/2 cup of tapioca flour, 1/4 cup of sorghum flour, 1 1/2 teaspoon of baking powder, 1 teaspoon of cinnamon (ground), 1/2 teaspoon of baking soda, 1/2 teaspoon of salt, 1/4 teaspoon of cloves (ground), 1/4 teaspoon of ginger (ground), and 1/4 teaspoon of nutmeg (ground) in a bowl. In a separate bowl combine the 1 can of pumpkin puree (15 oz), 3 eggs, 1/2 cup of brown sugar, 1/4 cup of butter (melted), and 1/4 cup of milk. Gradually add the dry ingredients into the batter, stirring until smooth. Fill each muffin cup to 3/4 and bake for about 27 minutes. Insert a toothpick into a muffin and if it comes out clean it is done. Set on wire rack to cool.

Meanwhile, mix the 1 1/2 cups of sugar (confectioners') with about 2 tablespoons of milk and 1/4 cup of melted butter, until it reaches a "drizzle" consistency. Add more milk if needed. Drizzle over the top of the muffins.

Stuffing

Stuffing goes excellent with turkey or chicken dishes. Makes 8 servings.

What You'll Need:

1 loaf of white bread (recipe in this book)
2 cups of chicken stock
2 eggs
1 1/2 cups of celery (diced)
1 cup of onions (diced)
3 tablespoons of olive oil
1 teaspoon of sage (dried)
1 teaspoon of thyme (dried)
3/4 teaspoon of salt
Pepper

How to Make It:

Prep: Preheat oven to 325 degrees Fahrenheit. Spray a 3 quart baking dish with cooking spray.

Cut the entire loaf of white bread into bite-sized cubes. Spread out onto a baking sheet and cook for about 14 minutes to toast.

Add the 3 tablespoons of olive oil to a skillet and turn to medium heat. Sauté the 1 1/2 cups of celery (diced) and 1 cup of onions (diced) for about 9 minutes. Sprinkle in the 1 teaspoon of sage (dried), 1 teaspoon of thyme (dried), 3/4 teaspoon of salt, and dashes of pepper and stir. Toss in the toasted white bread cubes. Crack and beat the 2 eggs and pour in with the 2 cups of chicken stock into the bread crumb mixture. Stir to soak the stock and transfer to the prepared 3 quart baking dish. Cover with foil and bake for half an hour in the hot oven, remove the foil and bake another 10 minutes. Serve warm.

White Bread

This is a classic loaf of bread, you can make sandwiches, toast or do anything with it you would with "wheat" bread. Makes 1 9x5 inch loaf.

What You'll Need:

3 eggs
1 1/3 cups of rice flour
1 1/4 cups of warm water
2/3 cup of sorghum flour
1/2 cup of cornstarch
1/2 cup of potato starch
1/3 cup of canola oil
3 tablespoons of sugar (granulated)
1 tablespoon of arrowroot
1 tablespoon of yeast (active dry)
1 1/2 teaspoons of salt

How to Make It:

Prep: Spray a 9x5 inch loaf pan with cooking spray.

Stir the 1 tablespoon of yeast (active dry) in the 1 1/4 cups of warm water. Add the 3 tablespoons of sugar (granulated), stir and set aside for about 7 minutes.

Crack and beat the 3 eggs and add to the yeast sugar water along with the 1 1/3 cups of rice flour, 2/3 cup of sorghum flour, 1/2 cup of cornstarch, 1/2 cup of potato starch, 1/3 cup of canola oil, 1 tablespoon of arrowroot, 1 tablespoon of yeast (active dry), and the 1 1/2 teaspoons of salt with a stand mixer (or hand if you don't have one) for 2 minutes on medium speed. Add the dough to the prepared 9x5 inch loaf pan, smoothing the top with damp fingers. Let dough rise for about an hour, it is ready when it puffs over the top of the loaf pan. Preheat the oven to 375 degrees Fahrenheit and bake for 25 minutes, until the top turns a golden brown.

Zucchini Bread

This is still the moist bread you loved without any wheat. Makes one 9x5 inch loaf.

What You'll Need:

3 eggs
2 cups of zucchini (grated)
1 cup of almonds (slivered)
1 cup of applesauce
1 cup of buckwheat flour
1 cup of raisins
1 cup of teff flour
1/2 cup of maple syrup
1 tablespoon of cinnamon (ground)
1 tablespoon of coconut oil (melted)
1 tablespoon of lemon zest
2 teaspoons of baking soda
2 teaspoons of vanilla extract
1 teaspoon of salt
1/4 teaspoon of baking powder

How to Make It:

Prep: Preheat the oven to 350 degrees Fahrenheit. Spray a 9x5 inch loaf pan with cooking spray.

Combine the 1 cup of buckwheat flour, 1 cup of teff flour, 1 tablespoon of cinnamon (ground), 1 tablespoon of lemon zest, 2 teaspoons of baking soda, 1 teaspoon of salt, and 1/4 teaspoon of baking powder in a bowl. In a separate bowl, beat the 3 eggs then combine with the 1 cup of applesauce, 1/2 cup of maple syrup, 1 tablespoon of coconut oil (melted), and the 2 teaspoons of vanilla extract using an electric mixer on low speed for a minute or two. Slowly add the dry ingredients and continue to mix with the mixer, only until the dry ingredients are moistened. Add the 2 cups of zucchini (grated) and the 1 cup of raisins. Place the dough in the prepared 9x5 inch loaf pan and bake for about 60 minutes, bread is done when a toothpick inserted in the middle comes out clean of batter. Cool on a wire rack in the pan for 10 minutes, then remove from pan and place back on the wire rack and finish cooling.

Wheat Free Diet Appetizer, Dessert, and Snack Recipes

Chocolate Pudding

This is a rich and creamy dessert perfect for chocolate lovers. Makes 6 servings.

What You'll Need:

2 cups of milk (divided)
3 egg yolks
3/4 cup of whipping cream
1/2 cup of sugar (granulated)
1/3 cup of cocoa powder
4 teaspoons of cornstarch
2 teaspoons of vanilla extract
1/4 teaspoon of salt

How to Make It:

Pour the 1 1/2 cups of milk into a heavy saucepan and stir in the 1/2 cup of sugar (granulated) and 1/3 cup of cocoa powder using a whisk. Turn to medium high heat and simmer. Take off heat once simmer starts. In a bowl, add the remaining 1/2 cup of milk with the 3 egg yolks, 2 teaspoons of vanilla extract, and 1/4 teaspoon of salt and stir using a whisk. Add the heated cocoa milk a little at a time, whisking continually to keep the eggs from cooking. Once all the milk is added to the egg yolks, pour it back into the saucepan and turn the heat to high, stir constantly with the whisk for another 2 1/2 minutes.

Either pour the pudding into a large serving bowl or 6 individual cups, cover with plastic wrap touching the pudding, and place in the refrigerator for several hours before serving. Make whipped cream by running a beater through the 3/4 cup of whipping cream for a couple of minutes. Garnish with a dollop of whipped cream.

Cocoa Macaroons

This is a delicious and easy cookie recipe. Makes 2 dozen cookies.

What You'll Need:

2 egg whites
1 cup of almonds (fine ground)
3 tablespoons of cocoa powder
1 1/2 cups of confectioners' sugar

How to Make It:

Prep: Preheat the oven to 400 degrees Fahrenheit. Line a cookie sheet with parchment paper.

Combine the 2 egg whites, 1 cup of almonds (fine ground), 3 tablespoons of cocoa powder, and 1 1/2 cups of confectioners' sugar. Use cold water to wet hands, then dip out about a teaspoon sized ball of dough, rolling it into a perfect ball. Place on the prepared cookie sheet. Bake in the hot oven for about 10 to 11 minutes. Allow to cool before removing and serving.

Five Layer Dessert Bar

This is a delicious dessert bar for those who enjoy coconut, chocolate, and nuts. Makes 2 1/2 dozen bars.

What You'll Need:

1 can of sweetened condensed milk (14 oz)
2 1/3 cups of coconut flakes (divided)
2 cups of peanuts (unsalted)
1 cup of semisweet chocolate chips
1 cup of butterscotch chips
1/2 cup of almonds (sliced)

How to Make It:

Prep: Preheat the oven to 350 degrees Fahrenheit. Spray a 9x13 inch baking dish with cooking spray.

Layer the bars by first laying 1 1/3 cups of coconut flakes on the bottom followed by the 1 cup of semisweet chocolate chips, 1 cup of butterscotch chips, and the 2 cups of peanuts (unsalted). Next pour the 1 can of sweetened condensed milk (14 oz) evenly over the top, covering all. Top with the 1/2 cup of almonds (sliced) and the remaining cup of coconut flakes. Bake for 20 minutes. Remove from oven, set pan on a wire rack to cool completely. Cut into squares when cooled and serve.

Fruit and Nut Cheese Ball

This is a different twist with a delicious cheese ball, made with pineapple and pecans. Makes 16 servings.

What You'll Need:

2 packages of cream cheese (8 oz each, room temperature)
2 scallions (chopped)
1 can of pineapple (20 oz, crushed, drained)
1 cup of celery (minced)
1 cup of pecans (chopped)
1/2 cup of bell peppers (green, chopped)
1/2 teaspoon of onion (minced)

How to Make It:

Combine the 2 packages of cream cheese (8 oz each, room temperature), 2 scallions (chopped), 1 can of pineapple (20 oz, crushed, drained), 1 cup of celery (minced), 1/2 cup of bell peppers (green, chopped), and 1/2 teaspoon of onion (minced) in a bowl. Form either a couple of small balls or one large ball. Roll the ball in the 1 cup of pecans (chopped). Cover and refrigerate for at least half an hour before serving.

Orange Cream Sorbet

This is a different twist on a cross between being a sorbet and a sherbet. Makes 8 servings.

What You'll Need:

1 package of Neufchatel cheese (8 oz, softened)
1 package of gelatin mix (3 oz, orange)
2 cups of whipped topping (frozen kind, thawed)
1 1/2 cups of boiling water
1/3 cup of frozen orange concentrate (thawed)
1 teaspoon of orange zest (grated)

How to Make It:

Stir the 1 package of orange gelatin (3 oz) mix with the 1 1/2 cups of boiling water until the gelatin dissolves. In another bowl, combine 1 package of Neufchatel cheese (8 oz, softened), 1/3 cup of frozen orange concentrate (thawed), and 1 teaspoon of orange zest (grated) with an electric mixer for a couple of minutes. Stir in the dissolved gelatin. Put in the refrigerator until it just begins to thicken (do not let it set!), keep checking every 15 minutes. Spray a 6 cup mold with cooking spray. Stir in the 2 cups of thawed whipped topping with the gelatin. Pour into the mold and refrigerate for a couple of hours before serving.

Peanut Butter Cookies

You will be amazed at the simplicity and ease of making these wheat free peanut butter cookies. Makes 3 dozen.

What You'll Need:

3 cups of peanut butter (creamy or crunchy, your choice)
3 cups of sugar (granulated)
3 eggs

How to Make It:

Prep: Preheat the oven to 350 degrees Fahrenheit.

Combine the 3 cups of peanut butter (creamy or crunchy, your choice), 3 cups of sugar (granulated), and the 3 eggs in a bowl. Drop by the spoonfuls onto a cookie sheet. Make criss cross patterns with the back of a fork. Bake for 8 minutes. Cool for 2 before removing to a wire rack for complete cooling.

Peanut Fruit Macaroon Sandwiches

This is a delicious cookie made with your favorite fruit jam. Makes 2 1/2 dozen cookies.

What You'll Need:

4 egg whites (room temperature)
2 cups of confectioners' sugar
1/2 cup of almond flour
1/2 cup of your favorite fruit jam
1/2 cup of peanuts (unsalted, roasted)
6 tablespoons of sugar (granulated)
1 teaspoon of vanilla extract

How to Make It:

Line a couple of cookie sheets with parchment paper. Add the 1/2 cup of peanuts in the food processor or blender and create fine ground nuts. Add the 2 cups of confectioners' sugar and the 1/2 cup of almond flour and continue to pulse, making a fine smooth powder. Run the powder through a sifter. Place the 4 room temperature egg whites in a bowl and beat with an electric mixer on high speed until peaks just start to form. Sprinkle in the 6 tablespoons of granulated sugar as you continue to beat. Stir in the teaspoon of vanilla extract and beat for a few more seconds. Using a rubber spatula, fold in small portions of the peanut flour, until it is all combined.

Place the mixture into a pastry bag with a star tip. Create 1 1/2 inch "cookies" on the lined cookie sheets. Meanwhile, preheat the oven to 375 degrees Fahrenheit. When the oven is hot, bake the cookies for about 14 minutes. Allow to cool with the parchment paper underneath on a wire rack before finishing. When all the cookies are baked, place a teaspoon of your favorite fruit jam onto the bottom of a macaroon and place a top macaroon over the jam, creating a sandwich. Serve immediately.

Salmon Spread

This is a perfect appetizer or snack to set out with gluten free crackers. Makes 3 cups.

What You'll Need:

1 package of cream cheese (8 oz, room temperature)
4 oz of smoked salmon (minced)
1/2 cup of sour cream
1 tablespoons of dill weed (minced, fresh)
1 tablespoon of lemon juice
Salt and pepper

How to Make It:

Using an electric mixer, add the 1 package of cream cheese (8 oz, room temperature), 1/2 cup of sour cream, 1 tablespoons of dill weed (minced, fresh), 1 tablespoon of lemon juice, and dashes of salt and pepper and mix until smooth on low speed. Stir in the 4 oz of smoked salmon (minced). Refrigerate for half an hour before serving.

Salsa with Black Beans

This makes a great addition to a Mexican meal or set out as a dip for gluten free chips or other vegetables. Makes 5 cups.

What You'll Need:

3 cans of black beans (15 oz, drained, rinsed)
2 cans of tomatoes with green chile peppers (10 oz, partial drained)
1 can of corn (11 oz, Mexican style, drained)
2 tomatoes (diced)
2 bunches of scallions (chopped)
5 teaspoons of cilantro leaves (chopped)

How to Make It:

Combine the 3 cans of black beans (15 oz, drained, rinsed), 2 cans of tomatoes with green chile peppers (10 oz, partial drained), 1 can of corn (11 oz, Mexican style, drained), 2 tomatoes (diced), 2 bunches of scallions (chopped), and 5 teaspoons of cilantro leaves (chopped) in a bowl. Set in refrigerator overnight before serving.

Spicy Nut Mix

This is a delicious snack for any time of day. Makes 4 cups.

What You'll Need:

1 cup of almonds
1 cup of peanuts
1 cup of pecans
1 cup of walnuts
6 tablespoons of brown sugar
4 tablespoons of butter
1 tablespoon of water
1/2 teaspoon of cumin (ground)
1/2 teaspoon of cayenne pepper
1/2 teaspoon of cinnamon (ground)
Salt and pepper

How to Make It:

Pour in the 1 cup of almonds, 1 cup of peanuts, 1 cup of pecans, and 1 cup of walnuts into a dry skillet on medium heat, stirring constantly for 5 minutes. Stir in the 4 tablespoons of butter and stir until melted then combine with the 6 tablespoons of brown sugar, 1 tablespoon of water, 1/2 teaspoon of cumin (ground),

1/2 teaspoon of cayenne pepper, 1/2 teaspoon of cinnamon (ground), and several dashes of salt and pepper. Stir and cook for about 5 minutes. Spread the nuts out on a foil lined baking sheet to cool. Bust apart with forks and store in a zipper bag or covered container at room temperature.

Wheat Free Side Dish Recipes

Boston Baked Beans

This is a delicious sweet and savory baked beans. Makes 6 servings.

What You'll Need:

2 cups of navy beans (dried)
1/2 pound of turkey bacon
1/2 cup of ketchup
1/2 cup of onion (fine chopped)
1/4 cup of brown sugar
3 tablespoon of molasses
1 tablespoon of Worcestershire sauce
1/4 teaspoon of dry mustard
Salt and pepper

How to Make It:

Sort and rinse the 2 cups of dried navy beans. Place in a bowl and cover with water and soak overnight. Drain the water and place the beans in a saucepan over high heat, bring to a boil, then turn to low and simmer for 90 minutes. Remove the beans from the water, save the water.

Preheat the oven to 325 degrees Fahrenheit. Place the beans in a casserole dish (2 quart) along with the 1/2 pound of turkey bacon and 1/2 cup of onion (fine chopped) and stir to combine. Add the 1/2 cup of ketchup, 1/4 cup of brown sugar, 3 tablespoon of molasses, 1 tablespoon of Worcestershire sauce, 1/4 teaspoon of dry mustard, and dashes of salt and pepper to a saucepan. Turn heat to high and stir continually until it comes to a boil. Immediately pour over the beans in the casserole dish. Use the reserved bean water; pour enough over the beans to cover all the beans completely with liquid, just cover, not too much. Seal the top of the dish with foil. Bake until beans are tender, for 1 hour and 45 minutes in the hot oven. Remove the foil cover and bake for another hour and 45 minutes, making sure the beans do not dry out. If the moisture dries up add a little more bean water.

Brown Rice Apple Salad

This is a different and unique side dish and a delicious light lunch. Makes 4 servings.

What You'll Need:

1 apple (granny Smith, cored, diced)
1 bell pepper (red, chopped)
1/2 bunch of scallions (chopped)
3 cup of brown rice (cooked)
1 cup of celery (chopped fine)
1/2 cup of walnuts (chopped)
1/4 cup of apple cider vinegar
3 tablespoons of olive oil
3 tablespoons of parsley (flat leaf, chopped)
2 tablespoons of lemon juice
Salt and pepper

How to Make It:

Combine the 1 apple (granny Smith, cored, diced), 1 bell pepper (red, chopped), 1/2 bunch of scallions (chopped), 3 cup of brown rice (cooked), 1 cup of celery (chopped fine), 1/2 cup of walnuts (chopped), 1/4 cup of apple cider vinegar, 3 tablespoons of olive oil, 3 tablespoons of parsley (flat leaf, chopped), 2 tablespoons of lemon juice, and dashes of salt and pepper in a large bowl by tossing. Refrigerate for half an hour then serve chilled.

Buffalo Chicken Breasts Salad

This is a perfect side dish with a main course of vegetables or as a lunch. Makes 4 servings.

What You'll Need:

2 chicken breasts cutlets
2 scallions (sliced)
8 cups of salad greens (your favorite salad greens)
2 cups celery (sliced thin)
1 cup of carrots (grated)
2 tablespoons of hot pepper sauce
1 3/4 tablespoon of blue cheese (crumbled)
1 1/4 tablespoons of buttermilk
1 1/4 tablespoons of yogurt (plain)
2/3 tablespoon of mayonnaise
1/3 tablespoon of vinegar (white)
2 teaspoons of olive oil
Pinch of sugar (granulated)
Salt and pepper

How to Make It:

Make the dressing by combining the 1 3/4 tablespoon of blue cheese (crumbled), 1 1/4 tablespoons of buttermilk, 1 1/4 tablespoons of yogurt (plain), 2/3 tablespoon of mayonnaise, 1/3 tablespoon of vinegar (white), Pinch of sugar (granulated), and dashes of salt and pepper with a whisk in a cup. Set in the refrigerator.

Preheat the boiler. Combine the 2 tablespoons of hot pepper sauce and the 2 teaspoons of olive oil in with a whisk. Cut the chicken cutlets into 1/2 inch strips lengthwise. Pour the hot sauce mixture over and evenly coat all pieces. Line a baking sheet with foil and place the chicken on the sheet. Cook under the hot broiler for 3 minutes, turn, and continue to cook for another 3 minutes.

In a large salad bowl toss together the 2 scallions (sliced), 8 cups of salad greens (your favorite salad greens), 2 cups celery (sliced thin), and the 1 cup of carrots (grated). Serve the salad on 4 plates, divide the cooked chicken on top of the salad, drizzle with equal amounts of the blue cheese dressing and serve immediately. Add extra dashes of hot pepper sauce if desired.

Candied Yams

Who says you can only enjoy yams on the holidays?
Enjoy this sweet yet highly nutritious dish any time of
year. Makes 8 servings.

What You'll Need:

1 can of yams (or sweet potatoes) (40 oz, undrained)
1/4 cup of brown sugar
1/4 cup of butter
Marshmallows

How to Make It:

Combine the 1 can of yams (40 oz, undrained), 1/4 cup
of brown sugar, and 1/4 cup of butter in a medium
saucepan. Turn heat to medium high and cook until the
liquid thickens and absorbs, about half an hour, stirring
often to prevent sticking.

Preheat oven to broil. Mash the yams with a potato
masher and pour into an 8x8 inch baking dish. Add the
marshmallows on top in a single layer. Place under the
broiler until the marshmallows melt, but not burn.
Serve immediately.

Fruit and Brown Rice Dish

This is a savory fruit flavored side dish that goes well with many main dishes. Makes 6 servings.

What You'll Need:

2 cups of chicken stock
1 1/2 cups of onion (sliced)
1 cup of cranberries (dried)
2/3 cup of mushrooms (fresh sliced)
1/2 cup of almonds (slivered, toasted)
1/2 cup of brown rice (uncooked)
1/2 cup of wild rice
3 tablespoons of butter
1 tablespoon of brown sugar
1/2 teaspoon of orange zest
Salt and pepper

How to Make It:

Combine the 2 cups of chicken stock, 1/2 cup of brown rice (uncooked), and 1/2 cup of wild rice in a saucepan. Turn the heat to high and bring to a boil, reduce heat to simmer, with lid on, for 45 minutes. Rice is done when it is tender and the stock absorbed. Add the 3 tablespoons of butter to a skillet on medium high heat.

Sauté the 1 1/2 cup of sliced onions and the tablespoon of brown sugar. Turn the heat to low and cook until the onions caramelize for about 20 minutes. Add the 1 cup of cranberries (dried) and the 2/3 cup of mushrooms (fresh sliced) and stir. Place a lid on the skillet and simmer for 10 minutes to rehydrate the cranberries. Add the 1/2 cup of toasted slivered almonds and the 1/2 teaspoon of orange zest and stir. Toss in some dashes of salt and pepper and serve immediately.

Healthy Collard Greens

Do not let the "healthy" stop you from enjoying this tasty side dish. Makes 8 servings.

What You'll Need:

1 bunch of collard greens (trimmed, rinsed, chopped)
6 cups of chicken stock
1 cup of turkey ham (chopped)
1 tablespoon of vinegar (white)
Salt and pepper

How to Make It:

Combine the 1 bunch of collard greens (trimmed, rinsed, chopped), 6 cups of chicken stock, 1 cup of turkey ham (chopped), 1 tablespoon of vinegar (white), and dashes of salt and pepper in a large saucepan. Turn heat to high and bring to a boil. Turn to low and simmer for an hour, stirring occasionally.

Oven Roasted Herbed Potatoes

This is a delicious side dish that goes with all kinds of meat and other vegetables. Makes 6 servings.

What You'll Need:

15 small potatoes (red new, scrubbed, dry with a paper towel)
1/4 cup of olive oil (extra virgin)
3 teaspoons of garlic (minced)
1 teaspoon of rosemary (dried)
Salt and pepper

How to Make It:

Prep: Preheat the oven to 350 degrees Fahrenheit.

Using a fork, poke holes all over the potatoes. Combine the 1/4 cup of olive oil (extra virgin), 3 teaspoons of garlic (minced), 1 teaspoon of rosemary (dried), and dashes of salt and pepper with a whisk. Add the scrubbed and dried potatoes with holes in the large bowl and coat all the potatoes. Place the potatoes in a shallow baking dish and bake until the potatoes are tender, about a half an hour to an hour.

Sautéed Spinach

What do you get when you combine spinach with garlic, butter and a sauté pan? A delicious side dish! Makes 4 servings.

What You'll Need:

1.5 pounds of spinach (baby leaves)
2 tablespoons of garlic (minced)
2 tablespoons of olive oil
1 tablespoon of butter
Lemon
Salt and pepper

How to Make It:

Run the 1.5 pounds of spinach (baby leaves) under cold water. Dry the leaves as best you can use a paper towel. Add the 2 tablespoons of olive oil to a large pot and sauté the 2 tablespoons of minced garlic, just long enough to heat, not brown. Stir in the dried spinach leaves, stir, and toss to coat with the oil and garlic. Add a hefty amount of dashes of salt and pepper and toss to coat. Cover and cook for a couple of minutes. Stir and heat through until the spinach leaves wilt. Toss in the tablespoon of butter. Serve with a dash of lemon juice and salt.

Seasoned Green Beans

This is a savory dish of garlic infused green beans.
Makes 5 servings.

What You'll Need:

2 cans of green beans (14.5 oz, drained)
1/4 cup of Parmesan cheese (grated)
3 tablespoons of olive oil
1 tablespoon of butter
3 teaspoons of garlic (minced)
Salt and pepper

How to Make It:

Combine the 2 cans of green beans (14.5 oz, drained),
1/4 cup of Parmesan cheese (grated), 3 tablespoons of
olive oil, 1 tablespoon of butter, and the 3 teaspoons of
garlic (minced) in a skillet on medium heat. Cook until
heated through, about 10 minutes. Stir in dashes of salt
and pepper and the 1/4 cup of Parmesan cheese
(grated).

Wheat Free Main Dish Recipes

Beef Stew

There is nothing quite as satisfying as a nice bowl of hot beef stew after a long day. Makes 6 servings.

What You'll Need:

2 pounds of beef stew
2 bay leaves
2 cups of water
1 1/2 cups of carrots (sliced)
1 1/2 cups of celery (chopped)
1/2 cup of onion (sliced)
2 tablespoons of canola oil
2 tablespoons of cornstarch
1 tablespoon of Worcestershire sauce
1 teaspoon of sugar (granulated)
1/2 teaspoon of garlic (minced)
1/2 teaspoon of paprika
Salt and pepper
Allspice

How to Make It:

Pour the 2 tablespoons of canola oil into a large pot and brown the 2 pounds of beef stew meat. Add the 2 cups of water, 1/2 cup of onion (sliced), 1 tablespoon of Worcestershire sauce, 1 teaspoon of sugar (granulated), 1/2 teaspoon of garlic (minced), 1/2 teaspoon of paprika, dashes of salt and pepper and allspice and stir. Add the 2 bay leaves, cover, and turn heat to low for 90 minutes. Discard the 2 bay leaves. Stir in the 1 1/2 cups of carrots (sliced) and the 1 1/2 cups of celery (chopped). Cover and cook for 35 minutes. If the liquid is not thick enough, remove 2 cups of the liquid and stir in the 2 tablespoons of cornstarch with a whisk. Pour back into the stew and stir. Continue to cook until it thickens to desired texture.

Chicken Enchilada Casserole

This is a delicious quick fix for an enchilada craving.
Makes 6 servings.

What You'll Need:

1 pound of chicken breasts (tenderloins, boneless,
skinless)
1 can of black beans (15 oz, drained)
1 can of tomato sauce (15 oz)
1 box of corn bread mix (7.5 oz, gluten free mix)
1 packet of taco seasoning
1 egg
1 cup of Mexican or fiesta style shredded cheese blend
1/3 cup of milk
1/4 cup of cream cheese (room temperature)
1/4 cup of water
1 1/2 tablespoons of chili powder
1 tablespoon of canola oil

How to Make It:

Prep: Preheat oven to 375 degrees Fahrenheit. Spray a
9x9 inch pan with cooking spray.

Combine the 1 can of tomato sauce (15 oz), 1 packet of

taco seasoning, 1/4 cup of water, and the 1 1/2 tablespoons of chili powder in a saucepan turn heat to medium. Pour the tablespoon of canola oil into a skillet and turn to medium heat. Add the 1 pound of chicken breasts (tenderloins, boneless, skinless) and brown on all sides, about 10 minutes. Stir in the tomato sauce mixture and simmer on medium low for about 8 minutes. Pull out chicken and shred with a fork and return to the sauce. Stir in the 1 can of black beans (15 oz, drained) and the 1/4 cup of cream cheese. Pour the chicken and sauce into the prepared 9x9 inch pan. Sprinkle the 1 cup of Mexican or fiesta style shredded cheese blend over the top. In a small bowl, combine the 1 box of corn bread mix (7.5 oz, gluten free mix), 1 egg, and the 1/3 cup of milk and spoon batter over the shredded cheese on the chicken. Bake until golden brown, about half an hour.

Chili

This is a slow cooked beefy chili, delicious and hearty, perfect for a cold winter day. Makes 8 servings.

What You'll Need:

1 pound of ground beef
2 cans of kidney beans (15 oz each, 1 drained, 1 undrained)
2 cans of tomato (10.75 oz, puree)
1 can of pinto beans (15 oz, undrained)
3/4 cup of celery (chopped)
3/4 cup of bell pepper (green, chopped)
3/4 cup of onion (diced)
1/2 tablespoon of chili powder
1 teaspoon of garlic (minced)
3/4 teaspoon of basil (dried)
3/4 teaspoon of oregano (dried)
1/2 teaspoon of parsley (dried)
Salt and pepper
Hot pepper sauce

How to Make It:

Brown the pound of ground beef in a skillet, drain the grease. Combine the cooked beef with the 2 cans of kidney beans (15 oz each, 1 drained, 1 undrained), 2 cans of tomato (10.75 oz, puree), 1 can of pinto beans (15 oz, undrained), 3/4 cup of celery (chopped), 3/4 cup of bell pepper (green, chopped), 3/4 cup of onion (diced), 1/2 tablespoon of chili powder, 1 teaspoon of garlic (minced), 3/4 teaspoon of basil (dried), 3/4 teaspoon of oregano (dried), 1/2 teaspoon of parsley (dried), and dashes of salt, pepper and hot pepper sauce in a slow cooker. Cover with a lid and cook on high for 4 hours or on low for 8.

Grilled Shrimp

This is a delicious marinated shrimp, which goes well with gluten free pasta or rice. Makes 6 servings.

What You'll Need:

2 pounds of shrimp (peeled, deveined, tails attached)
1 cup of olive oil
1/4 cup of parsley (fresh chopped)
2 tablespoons of hot pepper sauce
2 tablespoons of lemon juice
1 tablespoons of tomato paste
2 teaspoons of oregano (dried)
1 1/2 teaspoons of garlic (minced)
Salt and pepper

How to Make It:

Combine the 1 cup of olive oil, 1/4 cup of parsley (fresh chopped), 2 tablespoons of hot pepper sauce, 2 tablespoons of lemon juice, 1 tablespoons of tomato paste
2 teaspoons of oregano (dried), 1 1/2 teaspoons of garlic (minced), and several dashes of salt and pepper in a bowl with a whisk. Reserve about 1/4 cup of the marinade for later and pour the remainder in a gallon

size zipper bag. Add the 2 pounds of shrimp (peeled, deveined, tails attached) and seal. Shake the bag to coat all the shrimp and place in the refrigerator for 2 hours. Preheat the grill prior to cooking to medium low. Skewer the shrimp and discard the rest of the marinade in the bag. Spray the grate with cooking spray. Cook the shrimp for 10 minutes on the grill, basting with the reserved marinade. Turn once half way through, repeat with the basting.

Lemon Pepper Chicken

Lemon pepper has always been a favorite seasoning over chicken. Makes 4 servings.

What You'll Need:

4 chicken breasts (boneless, skinless)
1 lemon
1/4 cup of olive oil
1/3 cup of white grape juice
3 tablespoons of garlic (minced)
2 tablespoons of lemon juice
1 tablespoons of lemon zest
1 1/2 teaspoons of oregano (dried)
1 teaspoon of thyme (minced, fresh)
Salt and pepper

How to Make It:

Prep: Preheat the oven to 400 degrees Fahrenheit.

Add the 1/4 cup of olive oil to a saucepan and turn to medium-low heat. Sauté the 3 tablespoons of mince garlic for one minute, turn the heat off. In a separate bowl, stir in the 1/3 cup of white grape juice, 2 tablespoons of lemon juice, 1 tablespoons of lemon zest,

1 1/2 teaspoons of oregano (dried), and 1 teaspoon of thyme (minced, fresh). Add dashes of salt and pepper. Pour the liquid into a 9x12 inch baking dish. Rinse and dry the 4 boneless skinless chicken breasts. Coat the chicken breasts in the garlic olive oil. Then place them in the 9x12 inch baking dish and add more dashes of salt and a lot of pepper. Cut the lemon into 8 slices and place in the baking dish with the chicken breasts. Bake for 40 minutes, chicken is done when a meat thermometer reads 160 degrees Fahrenheit. Add more salt and pepper and serve.

Mushroom Broccoli Quiche

Quinoa is a great wheat substitute and works well as the crust in this delicious mushroom broccoli quiche. Makes 8 servings.

What You'll Need:

7 eggs
2 scallions (chopped)
2 cups of mushrooms (chopped)
1 1/2 cups of broccoli
1 1/4 cups of quinoa flour
2/3 cup of cheddar cheese (sharp, shredded)
1/2 cup of half-and-half
1/3 cup of butter (room temperature)
2 tablespoons of water
Salt and pepper

How to Make It:

Prep: Preheat oven to 350 degrees Fahrenheit. Spray a 9 inch pie pan with cooking spray.

Add the 2 cups of chopped mushrooms to a dry skillet on medium heat. Stir and cook for about 10 minutes. Add the 7 eggs to a bowl and beat with a whisk. Add the

1/2 cup of half-and-half and whisk some more. Stir in the 2 scallions (chopped), 2 cups of cooked mushrooms (chopped), 1 1/2 cups of broccoli, and dashes of salt and pepper. Add the 1 1/4 cups of quinoa flour in a bowl and mix with the 1/3 cup of room temperature butter. Mix until it is a good dough consistency. Add part of the 2 tablespoons of water, little at a time, until it reaches pie crust consistency. Press the dough into the sprayed 9 inch pie pan. Pour the egg mixture into the pie crust. Bake for 35 minutes until the eggs are set. Test by inserting a toothpick in the middle and if it's clean the eggs are set.

Oven Fried Chicken

This is a delicious want to cook "fried" chicken right from the oven. Makes 6 servings.

What You'll Need:

6 chicken breast halves (boneless, skinless)
1 cup of mayonnaise
1/2 cup of Parmesan cheese (grated)
1 tablespoon of rosemary (fresh chopped)
1 teaspoon of garlic (minced)
Salt and pepper

How to Make It:

Prep: Preheat the oven to 350 degrees Fahrenheit. Line a 9x13 pan with foil.

Combine the 1 cup of mayonnaise, 1 tablespoon of rosemary (fresh chopped), 1 teaspoon of garlic (minced), and dashes of salt and pepper in a bowl with a whisk. Spread the mixture over the top of the chicken. Sprinkle the 1/2 cup of grated Parmesan cheese over the top. Bake until the chicken is well done, when a meat thermometer reads 160 degrees Fahrenheit when inserted in the center of the thickest piece, about 70 minutes.

Salmon Packets

If you love salmon you will love, this super easy to cook recipe that almost contains a dinner in one packet. Makes 4 servings.

What You'll Need:

4 salmon fillets
1 can of tomatoes (14 oz, chopped, drained)
3/4 cup of onions (chopped)
2 tablespoons of lemon juice
2 tablespoons of olive oil
2 teaspoons of olive oil
1 teaspoon of oregano (dried)
1 teaspoon of thyme (dried)
Salt and pepper

How to Make It:

Prep: Preheat oven to 400 degrees Fahrenheit. Tear off 4 sheets of heavy duty foil, large enough to completely wrap each salmon fillet.

Drizzle the 2 teaspoons of olive oil over the top of the 4 salmon fillets. Sprinkle with dashes of salt and pepper. Lay a salmon fillet olive oil side down on each sheet of heavy duty foil. Bring the sides up to form a bowl with the foil. In a bowl combine the 1 can of tomatoes (14 oz, chopped, drained), 3/4 cup of onions (chopped), 2 tablespoons of lemon juice, 2 tablespoons of olive oil, 1 teaspoon of oregano (dried), 1 teaspoon of thyme (dried), and dashes of salt and pepper. Equally, spoon the tomato mixture over each salmon in foil. Seal the edges so the liquid and salmon remain inside. Bake in the hot oven for 25 minutes.

Stuffed Peppers

Rice and beef makes these peppers a delicious filling meal to enjoy. Makes 6 servings.

What You'll Need:

1 pound of ground beef
6 bell peppers (green)
2 cans of tomato sauce (8 oz)
1 cup of beef stock
1/2 cup of rice (long grain white, uncooked)
6 tablespoons of Parmesan cheese (grated)
1 tablespoon of Worcestershire sauce
1 teaspoon of Italian seasoning
1/4 teaspoons of garlic (powder)
1/4 teaspoon of onion (powder)
Salt and pepper

How to Make It:

Prep: Preheat the oven to 350 degrees Fahrenheit.

Pour the cup of beef stock into a saucepan and stir in the 1/2 cup of long grain white rice. Turn to high and bring to a boil, turn to low, add a lid and simmer for 20 minutes. Add the pound of ground beef to a skillet to brown it, drain the grease. Cut the tops off the 6 green bell peppers, remove all the spines and seeds, careful to leave the pepper intact. Place the peppers in a shallow baking dish, open ends up. Combine the cooked 1 pound of ground beef, 1 cans of tomato sauce (8 oz), 1 tablespoon of Worcestershire sauce, 1/4 teaspoons of garlic (powder), 1/4 teaspoon of onion (powder), and dashes of salt and pepper. Spoon evenly into the 6 bell peppers. Combine the remaining can of tomato sauce and the 1 teaspoon of Italian seasoning in a cup. Pour over the tops of the stuffed peppers. Place in the hot oven and bake for 60 minutes, basting with the seasoned tomato sauce every 15 minutes. Pull the dish out and sprinkle each pepper with a tablespoon of grated Parmesan cheese.

Conclusion

The success of the wheat free diet, or any diet for that matter, depends on the amount of effort you put into sticking with it. You have to view a diet as a complete change of lifestyle and not just something you will do for a week or a month or longer. If you are on this diet because of health issues such as a wheat intolerance, chances are you need to remain on the diet to alleviate the wheat intolerance symptoms indefinitely.

If you are on the wheat free diet to lose weight, be aware that you may very well lose the weight. However, the caveat is if you go back to the way you ate when you weighed more, the weight will pile back on. It is a fact, so you need to think in terms of completely eliminating the old way of eating. Even if you adapt the diet after you lose the weight, you must adapt it with healthy choices rather than going back to anything junky.

Healthy bodies require a lot of water, so be sure to drink plenty of water every single day. Healthy bodies require movement, so adopt an exercise routine, and work out several times a week for optimum results.

Last bit of advice - seek the counsel of your health care

provider before starting any new diet or exercise routine.

2310133R00060

Printed in Germany
by Amazon Distribution
GmbH, Leipzig